THE INSIDER'S GUIDE TO
CAR BUYING

**Tips and Tricks to Save You Money
and Protect Your Credit**

Phil Mendzat and Ryan Leverette

Tellwell Talent
www.tellwell.ca

ISBN
978-1-77941-390-1 (Hardcover)
978-1-77941-389-5 (Paperback)
978-1-77941-391-8 (eBook)

TABLE OF CONTENTS

PART FOUR
Your Credit and the Business Office 79

PART FIVE
Taking Ownership and After the Purchase 95

INTRODUCTION

We understand your fears when it comes to buying a vehicle. It is a huge purchase, usually only second to buying a home. So, of course, you are worried about getting taken advantage of, paying more than you should, or investing lots of money into a vehicle that is wrong for you.

No doubt you have also heard stories about how all car salespeople are liars and care nothing about you. Maybe you even know someone who has been taken advantage of. All of this just adds to the anxiety of buying a car from a dealership.

We understand your concerns. We have been where you are, looking to get a vehicle and worried about getting ripped off.

But a thousand times more, we have been on the sales end of the purchase and have helped thousands of people buy new and used vehicles.

We have also heard some of those horror stories from clients where things went wrong with their previous vehicle purchase, and they wonder if it is all going to happen again.

It didn't for them, and it does not have to happen for you.

Combined, we have worked in the auto sales industry for over two decades, and we have seen the good and the bad of the industry. So, you may want to ask us, "Is it true that dealerships try to rip you off and that car salespeople can't be trusted?"

For the large part, the answer is no. Dealerships are bound by laws and regulations that prevent them from trying to rob you of money, but they are businesses, and their goal is to make money. This means they may sell you a vehicle that is not the best deal for you; maybe the rates are too high, or the term is too long. Or it could be the result of one of many things that, while not illegal or immoral, are just not in your best interest. These things can cost you thousands and thousands of dollars and may hurt your credit.

But you can take a deep breath and relax. As we said, we have over two decades of experience in the car sales industry, and by the time you are done reading this book you will have the confidence to make a solid buying decision.

Because for the most part, vehicle salespeople are just like you. There may be a few less than ethical salespeople who are not above taking advantage of people, but truthfully, the biggest problem we see is people making uninformed decisions when it comes to buying a vehicle. It is a big purchase and doing it wrong can have a negative effect on your credit and finances.

But we'll show you how to avoid all these problems.

We both started our careers in the car industry in sales and advanced into management roles or different departments like internet sales and marketing. We have each worked at several different dealerships, where we have seen both the good and the bad of the industry. We have also worked with all kinds of sales reps, from all backgrounds and walks of life, and have learned which ones to work with and which ones to avoid.

We have also been on the other side of the table. We have both purchased vehicles from dealerships, and we understand what it feels like to be nervous about it. One of us had a great experience as he was already working in the auto sales industry and understood everything about what was going on. The other was young and had no idea what was happening. He believed what he was told by a less than reputable sales rep—the stereotypical "car sales guy"—and got screwed.

But, with our insider information, that won't be you.

There are many things dealerships will entice you with, such as 0% financing, no money down, and low payments over long terms. While these are all ethical and legal, they may not be the best thing for you and your finances in the long run.

So, this book is all about making sure that you not only get the best deal when purchasing your next vehicle, but also that the vehicle is right for you and you make the best decision regarding how to pay for that vehicle.

A vehicle is a need. We need a car to get to and from work, to get groceries, and to transport ourselves and our friends and family for recreational activities. Because it is such a necessity, it can be a stressful and intimidating purchase for people because they have heard all the stories about car salespeople and dealerships. While some may be accurate, most are like the fishing story that evolves from catching a nice-sized fish to a monster that took four hours to land.

But here is the good news! There are also a lot of great stories, too. In fact, there are way more good stories than bad ones. It is just unfortunate that when people are happy, they are nowhere near as loud as those who are unhappy. That's why you tend to only hear the bad news, which is a shame because buying a vehicle should be fun.

Yes, it's a big purchase, but it's an exciting one, and it can be a great experience. That's what we want for you. We want you to have a good experience and learn how to avoid the bad sales reps and dealerships.

The auto sales industry is not alone in its bad customer experiences. Dentists, doctors, lawyers, mechanics, carpet cleaners—people have good and bad experiences with all of them. The thing is, we tend to focus on the bad experiences and paint an entire industry with them. But it is not the entire industry that is faulty; it is only some of the people working in that industry.

What our experience has taught us is that there is a right way and a wrong way to buy a vehicle. Much of what you see online is the wrong way. Online, you are fed a lot of information by people who have never worked in the auto industry. They've had one bad experience and now they tell you, "How to beat the dealership," or "How to screw a salesman." It usually doesn't go so well for people that want to fight. After all, you catch more bees with honey. The people who have insider information and use it to work *with* the dealership and do so in a civilized and respectful manner are more likely to get the outcome they want.

Using insider information is having enough understanding about how car buying works and applying it to your buying habits so that you save money and protect your credit.

Everything we share with you is common in the car industry. Different dealers will have different terms or slightly different processes, but the economics and the systems are universal. To get into all the fine details and give examples of each would make you feel overwhelmed, but the good news is you don't need all that information. You just need to understand what all the basic options are and how they play a part in your vehicle purchasing habits. Then you can make an informed decision.

As we said, we have also been in your shoes. We've been through both bad and great vehicle-purchasing experiences and understand their long-term effects. In fact, one of us endured the classic nightmare car-buying scenario at a very young age.

Ryan Leverette's Story

I have been working in the auto sales industry for 15 years now. I started in sales and then developed an internet team at a dealership, was a sales manager at three other dealerships, and a general sales manager at another. I grew up in a town that had terrible public transportation. I had many miles to cover, and like many teenagers, I liked the freedom a car gave me. I liked being the one who could take my friends to different places and enjoyed having my own ride to work and school. I got my learner's permit when I was 14 years old and my driver's license a couple of days after turning 16. I already had a steady job while I was finishing high school, so I had saved up enough money to buy my first car, a 1990 Chevrolet Beretta and it served me well for two years.

Two years later when I turned 18, it was time to upgrade my wheels because the Beretta couldn't run any longer without some major mechanical work. I told my mom that I was going to go vehicle shopping and she thought I was going to buy another cheap car privately. Instead, I walked into a huge Chrysler dealership that was in the middle of town.

When I walked through the front door of that dealership, I was met by an older guy with black hair that was slicked back, lots of gold chains, gold pen, gold watch, and clothes about two sizes too small. He stuck out his hand to welcome me and looked at me like I was his next meal. I was young and didn't know better. Today, I'd recognize the red flags like the fact that he never took the time to get to know my needs or wants or my budget, he didn't really explain the purchase terms, and he barely went over the vehicle with me. I don't remember if we even went on a demo drive! Before I knew it, I was taking his word as gospel and signing a lease on a brand-new Dodge Dakota.

It was too expensive for an 18-year-old, and it wasn't long before I missed payments and hurt my credit. I went back into the dealership to see if there was anything they could do to help me change vehicles and lower my payments, but there was nothing they could do. My gold chain wearing sales rep had moved on suddenly, but a finance manager was kind enough to go over the fine details of the lease and tell me that I was stuck for the next four years. The worst part was that the Dakota was only rear wheel drive and not a 4 X 4 like the sales guy told me. So, I was stuck in a lease that I couldn't get out of, with a vehicle that didn't meet my needs and was damaging my credit score.

Now, was it my fault? Yes. I'm the one who signed the paperwork and walked out with the keys in my hand. The situation could have been avoided if I had been better informed, if I had known the red flags to look out for, and if I had read a book like this. Many years later when I entered into the car business and started selling cars, I swore I would never be like that guy who took advantage of me.

Do those guys still exist? Yes, but we will teach you how to avoid them.

We promise you, not all car-buying experiences end badly. Here's an example of a great experience that resulted in the purchase of a dream vehicle.

Phil Mendzat's Story

I love the rugged, wooded areas where I live, and I like to camp and hike. Because I worked at a dealership and was in a marketing position, I had the privilege of driving a demo vehicle, which is like a very cheap lease through the dealership. So, I had a new car to drive all the time. I would joke after a few months, "It's getting old, and it's close to having 500 miles. So, it's time for a new one." However, as it was a demo and could be sold at any time, I had to make sure it was clean and in good condition. I could not take my demo to all the places I wanted to go because there was a good chance it would get scratches and dents. I had always loved Ford trucks and dreamed about having one of my own that I could customize and take deep into the woods.

So, I treated myself like I would one of my clients. I went through my needs and wants list and how much I could afford. I considered what insurance, upkeep, and gas would cost me in a year and also what the long-term maintenance costs could be. It took a while to find it, but eventually I got my dream truck and now we go off on adventures together. Often, I come back from a weekend adventure and friends joke about seeing fresh scratches in the paint. For me, it's perfect: I can afford it, it meets my needs and wants, it's my baby, and I love her. Three years later, I still love that truck just as much as when I first bought it!

That's the kind of experience we want you to have. Find the perfect vehicle for yourself, your lifestyle, and your budget. This is the key to having a long, loving relationship with your vehicle, because no matter how sexy your ride is, if it kills you financially, the love is quickly gone.

The purpose of the first part of this book is to help you find a vehicle sales professional who can give you a great experience, just like we have given to thousands of clients.

These are the men and women who have built a great career based on treating people the way they would want to be treated. These are the people we want you to buy a vehicle from and we will show you how to find them.

We will also show you how to make sure the vehicle is right for you. Now, a good sales professional will be a huge part of this, but you also need to have enough savvy on your own to be able to make an informed decision. A vehicle is not only a huge purchase, but also one that you need to hold on to for at least a few years. So, let's make sure it's right.

The second part of this book will explain to you how dealerships work, how they make money, and the differences between them. Not all dealerships are the same, and this can affect how well you are taken care of in the event of a problem, the overall price of the vehicle, and other costs.

The third part of the book is for when you are ready to purchase a vehicle. We will explain how to get the best deal, the different options for purchasing and leasing that are often available, and how to get the most money for your trade-in vehicle. We'll also cover the differences between purchasing a new or used vehicle from a dealership.

The fourth part of the book covers the buying process—when you actually go into the business office. We'll go over some fundamentals about credit and interest rates, terms, and other things that sales reps will try to sell you at this time. We'll explain what they are and if they are a benefit to you.

Finally, the fifth part of the book is all about taking ownership of your vehicle and what you can expect after your purchase.

When it comes to purchasing a vehicle, it can be incredibly overwhelming. You will probably be offered a lot of things you are unsure about and don't understand. Relax. We are going to prepare you so you can make your purchase with confidence, and most importantly, we'll provide this information to you in a way that is easy to understand.

We want you to have the same great experience we provide for our clients, and we want you to love your vehicle long after the day you drive it off the lot. We also want you to be in a good financial position when you buy your car and not get stuck paying more than you should.

While we may not be able to have you as a client, our insider information will help you get the purchase experience you deserve.

PART ONE

Finding Your Sales Professional and Your Vehicle

"Car salespeople have one of the worst reputations for being sleazy, lying, and taking advantage of people, second only to telephone salespeople."

When I first went into vehicle sales, the dealership I worked at had a training program for people new to the industry, and we were told by our instructor that this was the general perception we would have to face.

Do you know what I said in response? I laughed and said, "Oh good. I am moving up. I was recruited from a telephone sales job."

OK. All joking aside, do you want to know if that stereotype is true? Of course, you do.

It is and it isn't.

But it's not just the car industry that has this problem. There are flakes and professionals in every industry, and it is always the unscrupulous few that give the rest a bad name. It's not the car sales industry that's the problem; it's just some of the people in it.

We have worked with plenty of sales professionals who are transparent—they answer all their client's questions and are completely honest with them because they know that they are building a book of business based on referrals. But we also know that there is the odd salesperson out there who will lie and do whatever is necessary to get the sale.

That's why a good vehicle-buying experience starts with the sales professional. We know it seems counter intuitive. You may think, "Surely it makes more sense to start by looking for the vehicle you want?" The fact is, ultimately, any real issues that arise are not a result of the vehicle, but of the person who sold it to you. Even if the vehicle is a lemon with all kinds of issues and problems, the fault lies with the person who either withheld that information or, if they didn't know about it, is not willing to help you out after the sale.

Any deceptions with regard to the actual cost of the vehicle are the fault of the sales professional who sold it to you. It's the same thing when someone tells you that a vehicle is right for you, but it's not because it does not fit your budget or lifestyle needs.

So, even if you know exactly what vehicle you want, don't go shopping for the vehicle, go shopping for a sales professional to sell you that vehicle. If you want a Ford, find a sales professional at a Ford dealership. Even if that dealership does not have the exact vehicle you want, chances are very good that a good sales professional can get it for you. Dealerships trade with one another all the time.

As we said, after a home, a vehicle is the second largest purchase that people make, yet when they buy a house, they enlist the help of a realtor. A realtor assesses your needs, wants, and budget and then uses his or her network to find the right home for you. You don't shop for the house first; you shop for a competent realtor first. It should be the same when buying a vehicle. Start with shopping for a good car sales professional.

The problem with following the vehicle first approach is that people will often buy a vehicle based on emotions and not the full picture. I mean, I want a Lamborghini, but I really can't afford one. Even if that's an extreme example, the irony is that there are ways of financing something like that whether you can afford it or not. Plus, there is the damage it does to your credit in the long term to consider.

A perfect example comes from when I was in my twenties and working in the oil and gas industry. It was a booming time and we made really good money. I mean really good money! A coworker of mine, who was the same age and making more money than he ever had in his life, wanted to buy a truck. A few days later he bought a top-of-the-line Ford Lariat truck with every possible feature short of ejector seats. He was proud at first and showed it off, but a few short months later he complained, "I don't own that truck; it owns me!" He told me that half his wages went to payments, and then another large part to insurance and gas. He was broke and now hated his truck.

Now, no laws were broken in selling the truck to this young person; he just made a bad decision that could have been avoided and unfortunately, he was stuck with it for a while.

A good sales professional will ask you about what kind of car you want—like what colors and features are in your dream car—but they will focus more on the unsexy questions like, how many kids do you have, how far will you drive, what will you use the vehicle for, and what is your budget.

A good sales professional understands how a vehicle purchase affects your life and your credit. He or she will say, "I get it, you want a Lamborghini, but it does not hold a car seat and you have a baby. Plus, the extra cost means you will be 'car poor' and you'll struggle to buy diapers."

The reason they do this is because they know that if they sell you something based purely on your emotions, they may get a deal in the short term, but it will cost them later. After a few months, when the reality of ownership kicks in— the insurance costs, the fuel costs, and how it just does not work for your day-to-day needs— you will hate them, bad mouth them, and never go back. This is the opposite of what they want. They want you happy, telling all your friends and family about your great experience, and coming back to them.

Good sales professionals also have more pull and more power than we ever give them credit for. They will know their inventory inside and out and be able to save you time by helping you select the right vehicle based on your needs and budget. If they don't have what you need, they can probably get it for you.

Good sales professionals will know what pre-owned vehicles are coming in that might not be on the website yet, and they can do a lot of the shopping for you by utilizing their knowledge and their network. They will be able to walk you through every step of the process because they are experts in everything from vehicle selection, to how to get the most money for your trade, to financing and leasing options. This is why you should always start with finding the right sales professional.

So, how do you find a good sales professional?

One of the best ways to find one is through a word-of-mouth referral. Recently one of our sales professionals got a call from a guy he didn't know who said, "My neighbor told me that he's bought lots of vehicles from you for his business. Can you help me get a truck?" Of course, he can. He's a pro! This guy gets referrals like this all the time because he makes sure that his clients are well taken care of.

So, who do you know who has bought a vehicle recently? Chances are that between your family, your friends, your coworkers, and even your acquaintances, more than a few have bought a vehicle in the last year or two. Talk to them about their experiences and if they were great, call the sales professional involved.

If you are having a bit of a challenge with this, then reach out on social media. Send a message on Facebook, Instagram, or whatever platform you use and just say, "Hey, I am thinking of buying a vehicle. Does anyone know a good car sales professional who can help me out?"

Then, once you have a name or two, have a look at online reviews. Look for sales professionals and dealerships that have consistently received great reviews. Now, reading online reviews is a bit of an art. Remember that those who complain are the loudest, and often the biggest complainers are just that, complainers. A good way to check this out is to look at reviews these people have left for other businesses. Click on the reviewer's profile and see what kind of reviews they are leaving for other companies.

The good reviews you want to look for are the ones that list what went well with both the dealership and the sales professional. Pay attention to the reviews that talk about an experience where the buyer's needs, wants, and budget were met, and where the buyer felt like the sales professional listened and provided proper help.

Reviews are not definitive, but they are an incredibly useful tool when shopping for your sales professional and dealership of choice. The key is to look for patterns of good reviews.

Another very good way to get an unbiased opinion is to call the dealership and talk to the receptionist. You can say, "A friend recommended a sales professional there to me, but I can't remember the name. My friend said that this person has been there for several years, is exceptional with clients, and makes sure that they are well taken care of. Because this person made sure that the whole purchase process was clear, my friend had a great experience." The receptionist will likely say, "Oh that sounds like—." And now you have a name. You could also simply ask the receptionist, "If you were buying a vehicle for yourself, who at the dealership would you buy it from?"

Now, here is a key tip: when you've found a sales professional you want to work with, book an appointment. The biggest annoyance for sales professionals is when people do not respect their time and think they are just sitting around doing nothing, just waiting for someone to walk in. In all the places we have worked, the really top people are very busy and often work by appointment only.

If you do just walk into the dealership without an appointment, you risk a few different things: You might have to sit there and wait for a long time to see the person you want to see. Or worse, you could get handed over to anyone who is free, and now you have no idea who you are dealing with.

Choosing a dealership or a vehicle based on good reviews will help, but choosing a sales professional with good reviews will help even more. The sales professional is the person you will interact with the most when you are shopping for and purchasing your next vehicle, and they will be the one you call if you have any issues after the purchase.

This is not to say that the dealership itself is not an important part of your vehicle purchase; it obviously is. However, our experience has shown us that good sales professionals do not stay at crappy dealerships. In fact, the best way to sniff out a bad dealership is by the sales staff turnover rate. You want to work with a dealership where the sales professionals have remained on staff for at least three years or more on average.

Another great way to sniff out a bad dealership is to look at its social media accounts. If a dealership does not have much of a social media presence or you see that there are always new salespeople featured each month, it's not a good sign. A good dealership that has kept sales pros around for a long time will have social media posts going back several years featuring the same sales professionals and their happy clients. That's a good sign.

But, determining if you have found yourself a good sales pro does not end with an online search. As you are meeting salespeople for the first time, learn to recognize the red flags that warn you they are not a real professional. Because even though you put some effort into finding a qualified professional, when you meet them in person, you may get the feeling that they are not as great as you hoped.

For example, I once did some secret shopping myself to see how the competitors were handling their clients. At one place, the guy I dealt with was the furthest thing from a professional. He never asked me about my needs or wants. We just test drove a vehicle because I liked the color. While we were on the test drive, he blatantly lied to me when I asked him about the truck's safety rating. He made up all sorts of things about how they rate safety and how they use a system up to forty points and this truck gets forty out of forty—a perfect score. There is no such safety rating, and I knew the truck did not have a perfect safety score. If I had been sincerely shopping for a vehicle, I never would have dealt with this guy.

The only good thing about this experience is that it is a perfect example of the kind of salesperson to avoid. They will try to get you on a demo drive right away rather than spending time getting to know your needs, wants, and budget. They won't know their inventory or how to do a proper qualification meeting, so they leave you sitting in their office or standing on the lot for long periods of time while they get their manager to do everything for them.

Pay attention to things like body language and tone of voice as well. Do they make you feel comfortable and taken care of with welcoming body language and a calm, confident tone of voice? Or are they standing around with their arms crossed looking all over the place nervously and talking too fast? A good sales rep will be knowledgeable enough to guide you through the process, but also will know when to get help. An unprofessional sales rep is either asking for help at every turn or just lying to you, making up answers to your questions just like I experienced. This is why you shop for a professional first and don't just walk into a dealership.

If for any reason you do not like the salesperson you are working with, even if he or she seems like a professional, just walk away and find someone else to buy a vehicle from. If you like the dealership you can ask to deal with someone else there. There is no crime in this. Vehicles are not cheap and in reality, the vehicle-purchasing experience is about you and your needs. Yes, you should like your sales professional, but you are not buying from them just because of this. A true sales professional will focus on you and your needs above and beyond anything else.

Once you have found your sales professional, it's time to shop for vehicles. Buy a vehicle the same way you would buy a house. In other words, have a rough idea of what vehicle you are interested in and what your budget is, and do a bit of research. Research can help you in case you run into a guy like I did, and he lies to you. Clearly communicate to your sales professional what research you've done on vehicles, your needs and wants, and your budget. Let them know up front if you have a trade-in, how much money is left owing on it, and the condition it's in. Let them know if you plan on paying cash or if you will need financing or leasing options, and how strong or weak your credit situation might be. Then, let them go to work! Let them utilize their network and expertise to put vehicles in front of you that meet your requirements. Let them tell you the history and important notes about the vehicles. Let them help you get the most money for your trade-in. Let them explain your financing and leasing options. Let them help you with finishing up paperwork and the insurance and delivery process.

When you choose your sales professional first, you will have a better purchasing experience, save a lot of time and headaches, and probably save a lot of money as well.

"Wait. A good sales professional will save me money?!"

Yes! For starters, time is money, and they will save you a lot of time. They are ultimately intermediaries working on your behalf—brokers if you will. If they don't get you the deal you want, they aren't selling a car and they aren't making a paycheck. Additionally, a good sales professional thinks long term. Yes, they all want to sell you a car, but they are thinking long past one sale. This isn't a job for them. It's a career, and a career isn't built off of one deal. They want you to come back and purchase your next five cars over the next twenty years from them. They want you to have a great experience because they know you will talk about it when you are showing off your new ride, and this will get them more clients too. A good sales professional wants to earn your trust and patronage long term.

Another key indicator of a good sales professional is that they own up to their mistakes right away and work hard to fix them. Vehicles aren't perfect. They come with thousands of moving and non-moving parts. Every once in a while, something is bound to go wrong. Maybe the original equipment manufacturer window sticker was misprinted or perhaps an accessory item you ordered with your vehicle is backordered when it was promised to be in stock. Mistakes happen, but a professional will take responsibility for the mistake and get involved. They don't make you feel alone after you've purchased the vehicle and hide behind paperwork, nuances, or managers. They have a vested interest in making sure that your experience after the sale is just as good as your experience during the sale.

In closing, buy a vehicle the same way you would buy a home. Choose your sales professional first and communicate clearly and honestly with them. Always book an appointment, even if it is a phone or video call. Respect their time and they will respect yours. Trust them and they will give you a great experience while saving you time and money.

HOW TO DO A PROPER TEST DRIVE

The demo drive is one of the most important parts of purchasing a vehicle. This is your chance to really feel the vehicle and make sure it meets your needs and wants. It should also be fun! What's the point of vehicle shopping if you don't get to drive a few vehicles? Enjoy it!

Contrary to popular belief, we suggest taking the sales professional with you on the demo drive, at least the first one. Remember, the sales professional is your ally, and you want them with you and on your side.

When doing a demo drive, there are a few things to keep in mind. Imagine that you are in the market for a lightly used sedan, and you book an appointment to view a three-year-old Honda Accord. Since the car is pre-owned, the dealership should have completed a safety inspection and done some reconditioning to the car already, but what if they missed something? Imagine that you go for a demo drive, and you hear a bad clunking noise coming from the front driver's side wheel, or the brakes shudder when you apply them.

You want the sales professional with you so that they notice it too. With the sales professional at your side, they might suggest a different vehicle altogether. Or they can help get the vehicle through a secondary safety inspection or whatever it takes to rectify the issue, so it won't cost you in the end.

With new or pre-owned vehicles, the sales professional will be able to answer your questions and further explain the features of the vehicle while you are on the demo drive. Nowadays, vehicles come with a lot of technology and there are probably new things you do not know about, and many features can only be experienced while you are driving the vehicle. So, allow your sales professional to give you a full presentation of the car before you go on a demo drive. On the demo drive, they can answer any other questions that you may have.

Lastly, you want your sales professional to accompany you on the demo drive so that you maintain the relationship with them throughout the entirety of the purchasing process. If you've done the right thing and chosen your sales professional ahead of time, this will likely be someone who is a good person that you will get along with. Have fun on the demo drive. Laugh and make a friend. As you get to know each other, you will build trust, and it's more likely that the purchase after the demo drive will go smoothly.

Here are some key things to keep in mind when actually doing a demo drive. First, make sure you're comfortable. Being comfortable means being safe. It means you can actually focus on the vehicle and how it feels and drives instead of the fact that you can't reach the pedals or see out of all the mirrors. Adjust the seat first, then your side mirrors and rearview mirror. Adjust the climate control so that the cabin is comfortable. Turn the radio off so it is not a distraction and, more importantly, you can actually hear the vehicle. If the stereo is important to you, stop at some point and test it out. Simply put, these are not things you want to have to think about while you are navigating traffic in a vehicle that is unfamiliar to you.

Drive a few city roads and a few highway roads if possible. Most vehicles won't show signs of excess wear and tear under speeds of 50 miles (80 kilometers) per hour. Make sure you are going somewhere where you can get the vehicle

Adjust to suit you before test drive.

"up-to-speed." Drive like you would normally drive so you can feel everything about this vehicle. Pay attention to the way the vehicle feels at slow speeds and fast speeds. Pay attention to the way the vehicle handles bumps and turns. Don't avoid bumpy roads. Go for them! Drive up and down hills. Is the cabin exceptionally noisy? Are there weird noises coming from any part of the vehicle? How is the acceleration and handling? Do the tires slip at all? Does the steering wheel or any other part of the vehicle shake excessively? Do the brakes shudder when you apply them, or do they feel safe and solid? You get the idea. And this is not just for pre-owned vehicles; it applies to new ones as well.

Sometimes, you'll come back from your first demo drive and just know that this is the right vehicle for you. If that's the case, proceed with confidence and have fun purchasing your new vehicle. However, sometimes one demo drive is not enough. This is a big, expensive decision and most demo drives are only 10–15 minutes long. This might not be long enough for you to fully experience the vehicle. If you decide to take a second demo drive, we suggest doing the drive alone so that you can really take your time. This is also a great way to respect your sales professional's time and keep them on your side.

Ask your sales professional if they can sign the vehicle out to you for a few hours, or maybe even overnight. Drive the vehicle like you own it. No, don't see how far you can jump the car or how well it does a burnout, but drive it in everyday life scenarios. Go get some groceries. Drive it to and from your workplace to see how it will feel during your daily commute. Take it on the highway and drive out of town a bit. Throw your car seats in it and take the kids for lunch. Park it in your driveway or garage and make sure it fits!

A vehicle has to fit you and your lifestyle in so many ways and the test drive is the trial run to make sure it does. Take your time.

PART TWO

How Dealerships Work and How They Make Money

When it comes time to buy your car, knowing how dealerships work and how they make their money will give you the power to get the best deal you can.

This section will outline the costs a dealership has to cover and how that affects the price of the vehicle you want to buy. We'll also get into the different people, other than the sales pro, who you will be working with and what part they play in your vehicle purchase.

We'll also talk a little about the different kinds of dealerships you can buy a vehicle from and the huge difference that can make, especially with a used vehicle.

THE THREE WAYS A CAR DEALERSHIP MAKES MONEY

There are typically three ways dealerships make money. Parts sales, vehicle servicing, and vehicle sales.

The most consistent parts of the business are the parts and service departments. Dealerships call parts and servicing, "fixed operations."

The most inconsistent, but potentially most profitable part of the business is vehicle sales. Dealerships call vehicle sales, "variable operations."

Most car dealerships aim for something called "absorption." This is when the parts and service departments are profitable enough to cover all of the overhead of the business, leaving the variable operations, car sales, for pure profit.

That profit can vary significantly depending not only on how much they sell a vehicle for, but also how the purchaser pays for it. Many still think that paying cash will get them the best deal. It won't, because the dealership also makes money on what is called the "back end" of the car deal. This is money that is made off financing, maintenance plans, and other things that come with buying a vehicle. We'll cover these things and whether they are good for you in the next part.

WHAT IS A DOCUMENTATION FEE AND IS IT LEGITIMATE?

The infamous documentation fee. Let's talk about it.

Some dealerships have other names for it, such as an admin fee, but really, it's all the same.

A documentation fee, or doc fee for short, is what dealerships add to the sale price of a vehicle at the time of purchase to help cover overhead costs, and it can vary from a few hundred to over a thousand dollars depending on the dealership.

There is a lot of debate as to whether the doc fee is legitimate or something that dealerships do to just pad their pockets. But after over two decades in the car sales industry, we can tell you that it is legitimate. Some argue that dealerships overinflate the doc fee or abuse it, but very few of them do.

Typically, the documentation fee covers three things.

1) It's an operational overhead fund. It helps cover the costs of running the building itself: the electrical bill, the land lease, the heating bill, etc.

2) It actually does cover some of the documentation costs, such as facilitating paperwork, software expenses, lien checks, and the added cost of storing files for a minimum of seven years. Trust us. That is a lot of paper and files!

3) It helps cover the cost of hourly support staff that make your experience at the dealership better. These are people like the reception staff, vehicle detailers, custodians, and so on.

This is a generalization, but we have seen the accounting books of several dealerships, and these three categories are largely supported by the documentation fee.

This also explains the differences in documentation fees. A used car dealership that has a small building, not a lot of paperwork to facilitate, and limited support staff will usually have a smaller doc fee. A new premium car dealership that has a big fancy building, lots of paperwork to facilitate, and lots of support staff will usually have a larger doc fee.

We have seen dealerships with full coffee bars, business centers, and even nail salons and golf simulators available for customers to use for free while they are in the dealership. The bigger dealerships typically also have better concierge services such as service vehicle pickups and drop offs. But the fancier the dealership, the higher the doc fee.

So, if you prefer to deal with a dealership with lots of support staff and other things, be prepared to pay a higher doc fee. If those things are not important to you, then you would probably be happier going to a smaller, less fancy dealership and paying a smaller doc fee.

In most states and provinces, dealerships are required to properly advertise their documentation fee either on the website or on the vehicle window sticker itself, or both. If it's not properly advertised and disclosed, don't pay it. It should not just randomly show up on your sales worksheet or bill of sale. It must be properly advertised.

Usually, if customers are turned off by having to pay a documentation fee, it is because it came as a surprise. Buy from a reputable dealership that clearly advertises their documentation fee and know why you're paying it.

THE COST OF INSPECTIONS AND WHY DEALERSHIPS HAVE TO DO THEM

I f you are looking to buy a used car, this is really important as it affects the cost and also the reliability. If you are going to trade in a vehicle when you buy a new one, it will also help you understand how the dealership appraises the value of your trade-in.

Car dealerships have to inspect used vehicles before they sell them to ensure their safety, reliability, and legality for resale. It also helps to identify any necessary repairs or maintenance requirements before selling the vehicle. If a vehicle needs a lot of expensive repairs, they may decide to "wholesale" the vehicle to an authorized buyer and not to the public. They will not sell a vehicle like that to the public, as there can be a lot of problems legally down the road for the dealership. In addition to complying with state or provincial regulations, it also helps protect the dealership's reputation and builds customer satisfaction.

Dealing with independent dealers can be a very gray area and laws can vary greatly from state to state and province to province. Mostly, we would recommend avoiding buying a used car from these types of dealerships. These places will only deal in used vehicles, generally do not have a mechanical shop attached, and typically do not offer anything in the way of a guarantee. If something catastrophic goes wrong, it is doubtful they will help you out in any way. Even if a vehicle passes inspection, there is no guarantee that you will not encounter a major repair after buying it. I personally have bought privately and from independent dealerships and, even after getting the cars inspected elsewhere, I've been stuck with expensive repairs after a few months. This is the risk of buying privately or from an independent dealer. This does not mean they are bad, but there is more of a gamble at stake.

Generally speaking, we recommend buying your pre-owned vehicles from a reputable major manufacturer dealership such as Ford, Kia, Chrysler, Lexus, Nissan, etc. They will readily have inspection reports available and a reputation to maintain.

Now, independent dealers will often have amazing deals, and this can be enticing, but the reason is often because the vehicle has been in a massive accident and has been reconditioned. This means they will take a vehicle that has been salvaged and resell it.

A salvage vehicle is a vehicle that has been in an accident and the insurance company has decided that the cost to fix the damage outweighs the value of the vehicle. If a vehicle that is worth $12,000 has $18,000 worth of damages to fix, the insurance company will decide that it is not worth fixing, and they will deem it a write-off. The vehicle is typically taken to a wrecking yard to be destroyed, but, in some cases, the vehicle is auctioned off or sold to a broker. The places that purchase these vehicles do so at a very low cost and they either use them for parts, or they fix them and resell them. Typically, these shops do the work in-house for cheap and fix only what is needed to make the vehicle drivable again. Sometimes the vehicle is totally safe—and sometimes it's debatable.

When I was younger, I sustained a knee injury that required surgery. The surgeon did a great job, and I regained use of my knee again. However, as I get older, it's just not the same. The damage has been done, and my knee will never be the same again. My knee is technically repaired, but it requires a little extra work and maintenance than normal to keep it in good condition.

The same goes for a salvage vehicle. It may be a deal in the short run, but chances are there will be some major problems later. The car may have been repaired, but it will likely never be the same again and probably will require more maintenance and future repairs than other vehicles.

When you buy from a franchised dealership, you will pay a bit more for the unit. But with that extra cost comes the reassurance that the vehicle has been properly inspected and that any work that was necessary has been done. The vehicle will be ready to insure and drive. Many used vehicles that are only a few years old may have some sort of warranty remaining as well, and extended warranty options are likely to be offered.

When any dealership sells a used vehicle, they must declare to you any accidents the vehicle has experienced or repairs that they have carried out. This is why it is very important to make sure you see the CARFAX Report, or insurance history report, for any pre-owned vehicle you are considering. In most provinces and states, dealerships are required to tell you about any previous accidents or insurance claims. If a dealership is not willing to show you the insurance history report, that's a massive red flag. Run away.

Whether you buy a pre-owned vehicle from a reputable major manufacturer dealership, an independent dealership, or privately, once you pay for the vehicle, sign the paperwork, and drive away, it's yours. Make sure you take the time to know its history and what work has been done on it.

THE ROLE OF THE SALES PROFESSIONAL

This is the person who will help you find a vehicle and the one who will be there through the whole vehicle-buying process. The sales professional is the person you will build the closest relationship with at the dealership, and he or she will often act as a first point of contact for other things you may end up needing later.

Sales professionals are the front-line employees; their job is to sell you a vehicle. Some sales roles at dealerships are a hybrid where the salesperson gets a base wage plus commissions, but the vast majority are paid on commissions alone. Sometimes, in a hybrid position they may calculate different payment options for you, but generally this is the sales manager's job.

When it comes time to buy, they act as a go-between for you and the sales manager, who will provide the value of your trade-in and calculate different payment options for you to buy your new vehicle. The sales pro will also take any counter offers or any other adjustment you'd like to try and make to the sales manager on your behalf. They typically do not have the authority to say yes or no to requests you make, but they are the ones that will go to bat for you and try to get the sale, because that is how they make their living.

THE SALES MANAGER ROLE

The main goal for a car sales manager is to help their team set and hit sales targets. Managers will also provide support, coaching, and motivation to their teams. They set payment plans and implement sales strategies. Their main objective, however, is to help the sales professionals sell cars.

They are the ones who your sales professional will take all your offers and requests to, and they are the ones who put together different payment options and plans for you. You may interact with a sales manager a bit during the car purchase process, but they do more work behind the scenes.

Sales managers often deal with a lot of issues after the sale, like if there is some problem with your vehicle, but your sales professional will likely still be your first point of contact for those issues.

THE GENERAL SALES MANAGER OR GSM

A general sales manager at a car dealership is the boss of the sales managers, service managers, and the sales team. They will spend most of their time working with the sales managers and they oversee the operations of the dealership. They make sure the dealership is selling enough cars and making enough money and they work out strategies for the dealership sell more cars and make more money. Overall, they keep an eye on what's going on in the market, the dealership, and with the customers. They are responsible for liaising with the vehicle manufacturer and other supporting companies that make the dealership run.

Primarily, the general sales manager will interact with people in a management position at a dealership. The general sales manager often coaches and guides the sales managers in dealing with customers and staff to resolve issues and problems, but the majority of their time is spent managing the logistics of running a dealership.

Whether or not you will meet the general sales manager has a lot to do with the type of dealership you are dealing with and its work culture. If the general sales manager comes out to greet you as you are purchasing a vehicle that is a great sign. But if it doesn't happen, do not be alarmed. The general sales manager is dealing with a lot—and we mean a lot.

THE FINANCE MANAGER

This is the person you will meet with once you have chosen a vehicle and are ready to set up the financing or payment. The finance manager will be the one who goes to different lending institutions to get you the best interest rate and will cover everything to do with your vehicle loan and financing. They will do a check on your credit history to see what kinds of interest rates and terms they can get for you; they will also try to sell you additional warranties or packages for your car.

PART THREE

Buying Your Vehicle and How to Get the Best Deal

Wow! Congrats. You have found a great ride and are ready to buy a vehicle. Now you will be presented with different options regarding payments, lease vs. finance, length of terms, and so on depending on your credit and the vehicle you are purchasing.

This part of the book will not only show you how to get the best deal, but also how to make sure that buying the vehicle helps and does not hurt your credit. Because if you get a good price on the vehicle but end up paying thousands more than you should in interest, or end up buying things you don't need, then it wipes out the fact that you got a good price on the car.

While we are not financial advisors and we are not licensed or bonded to give you financial advice, we do have a lot of experience in car sales and so we also have a good understanding of how credit and financing works. The information here is generally related to how financing a vehicle and credit affect one another; however, there are also many other factors that have an impact on a person's ability to finance a vehicle, such as a recent bankruptcy, divorce, or many other things that happen in life that change an individual's credit situation.

What we will share with you will help you make an informed decision and give you a better understanding of how different things affect your credit. Too often we have seen clients with damaged credit and not in the best position to buy a new car because they did not receive good advice on how to properly buy and finance their previous car. We don't want that happening to you.

We'll also tell you about all the different options or promotions that may be presented to you and show you how they work. This way, you will be able to judge if they might be good for your situation or not.

HOW TO ACTUALLY GET THE BEST PRICE

This is simple. The best way to get the best price is to be ready to buy—actually ready to buy. When you are no longer shopping, but ready to purchase, you will get the best price.

People who get the best price are always in a position to make a purchasing decision right away, if not the same day. Make sure that's the position you're in before you start asking for the best price or the best deal.

Why? Because dealerships are motivated by time. They want to earn your business. The majority of the people working at the dealership from the sales pros—who are mostly on a 100% commission pay plan— to the sales managers and the finance managers only get paid when you buy a vehicle. So, if you are ready to buy, they are ready to deal.

Your commitment to purchase is what motivates the dealership the most. Use it to your advantage, but don't say you are ready to commit when you're not.

Many times, people have said, "I need to think about it" or "I need to talk to my spouse" or they list other reasons for why they do not want to buy that day. If you need to do something like this, do not take more than a day or two to get back to your sales professional.

What often happens is they take too long to come back and then are angry that they are not getting the same payment plan or interest rate or that the vehicle is no longer available.

Offers, rebates, discounts, and interest rates change from month to month at a dealership, and dealerships have no idea what the new offers will be until the beginning of the next month. So, when your sales professional tells you that they can't promise you the prices if you wait too long, they are telling you the truth, especially if it is the last day of the month. They don't know what incentives or deals are coming next week or next month. Only the manufacturers do, and they don't tell the dealers until the first of the month. Even if a dealership is offering their own incentives, they're likely to change often.

When it comes to pre-owned vehicles, most dealerships price according to the market and supply and demand. Other dealerships selling similar makes and models can cause your dealership to lower or even raise the price of their pre-owned vehicles frequently—even daily.

When I worked as a used-car sales manager, I used to look at each vehicle in our pre-owned inventory daily. I would assess how many similar models were on the market and what they were selling for. I would compare my inventory to what other local dealerships had and what they were selling at. All this meant that I was constantly adjusting prices up and down on the pre-owned vehicles at my dealership. Prices changed at least every week and sometimes on a daily basis.

Interest rates are affected by what the big banks do. In Canada, new and used vehicle interest rates will raise and lower in relation to the Bank of Canada. Therefore, if we knew that the Bank of Canada could be raising the prime rate soon, we would encourage our customers to lock in the lower interest rates that were currently available. This isn't a sales tactic to get you to buy sooner. More often than not, it's the truth. A good sales professional is looking out for your best interests.

One secret tip that can help you negotiate a better deal is to purchase your vehicle closer to the end of the month. Sales professionals, sales managers, and dealerships have quotas that they need to hit each month. If they are a bit behind at the end of the month, they will have more incentive to earn your business and you could end up with a better deal.

LEASING

What is a lease?

Some people refer to leasing as renting a car from the bank. It's not. It's just a different way of purchasing a vehicle. Rather than purchasing the whole vehicle, you only purchase part of it for the time that you are using it. This generally happens for 24, 36, or 48–month terms.

During this term, you are only making payments on a predetermined portion of the vehicle for a predetermined period of time. At the end of a lease, you typically have three options available to you:

- You can return the car to the dealership and walk away as long as you have maintained the vehicle properly and are within the minimal wear and tear guidelines and kilometer restrictions set out at the beginning of the lease.

- You can buy the car for the pre-determined residual value set out at the beginning of the lease.

- You can use the vehicle as a trade towards another vehicle. (Terms and conditions of using a lease for trade-in vary greatly. Ask your sales pro for more details.)

If you are someone who likes to change vehicles every few years, leasing is a great option for you, as you do not risk having to roll money owed on a trade into a new vehicle. Leasing can also be a better tax write-off for people with businesses, but that is something to discuss with your accountant.

Because you are only paying for a portion of the vehicle, you do not pay the full manufacturer's suggested retail price (MSRP), and you also pay less in taxes. It also means that it can be a little easier to lease a new vehicle vs. financing it, because you are applying for credit on a lower amount of money.

The downside of a lease is that the car is not yours and at the end of the lease term, you must either turn it in or buy it. If you choose to buy, it is the same as buying a used vehicle, so you will have a shorter term and higher interest rate than you would for a new vehicle.

A lease also limits how many miles or kilometers you can put on the vehicle. So, it's bad for people who drive a lot and put lots of miles on their car. Since you cannot make a lot of modifications or add certain accessories to a leased vehicle, it's definitely not a performance or off-road choice. Most leases will have a lease-end financial penalty for putting more than the allotted mileage on a vehicle and for any extra repairs or reconditioning the vehicle might need at the end of the lease, and these penalties can be substantial.

Some leases restrict where you can use the vehicle. You may end up paying a penalty or the leasing company may repossess your vehicle if you move to a different province or state than where the lease was negotiated.

But, for most car owners, leasing is a viable option that is often better for them than financing. So, let's look at how leasing vs. financing works.

With a lease you are not paying for a whole vehicle, only the portion you use. So as an example, let's look at a 48-month lease on a new Jeep Wrangler Unlimited Sahara with an MSRP of $68,288. The manufacturer has set a residual value of 52% of the MSRP based on driving 12,500 miles (20,000 kilometers) per year over a four-year term with average wear and tear. This means the Jeep Wrangler will be worth $35,509, 52% of the MSRP, at the end of four years, provided it has less than 50,000 miles (80,000 kilometers) and average wear and tear.

With a lease like this, your payments are based on 48% of the value of the Jeep. So, rather than making financing payments on $68,288 plus fees, taxes, and interest, you are making payments on $32,799 plus fees, taxes, and interest.

Since the manufacturer or the leasing company set a predetermined residual value, also called a predetermined trade value, you know exactly what your vehicle will be worth at the end of the lease term.

Many people have a bad experience with getting less for their trade-in value when they go to buy a new car. But with a predetermined trade-in value, you get the amount that was agreed upon, assuming there is no damage and you do not exceed the maximum mileage.

For example, let's say it's time to trade in the Jeep Wrangler with a preset value $35,509, but things have changed in the marketplace and the dealership says it has an actual cash value of $31,509.

Well, the manufacturer who set the predetermined price has to eat that difference. You are not required to make up any difference in value.

If you've fallen in love with the Jeep, you can decide if you want to buy it out for $35,509 or walk away from it.

If the market is up and the value is determined to be higher than the predetermined trade value, say $38,509, then you have $3,000 of equity that can be applied towards a new lease if you want to lease a new vehicle.

Additionally, you could ask your local dealership if they'd like to buy the vehicle from you and pocket $3,000 of cash.

Another benefit to leasing relates to your credit bureau. Leasing is a great option for people who want to keep their borrowing to a minimum but still want to drive a nice vehicle. How is that? Because when you lease a vehicle, the manufacturer or leasing company will only report to your credit bureau the portion of the vehicle that you are using, not the full MSRP.

Maybe you have already applied for an automotive loan and the bank has told you that, based on your current credit rating, they will only lend you $32,799, not the $68,288 you would need for that new Jeep Wrangler Unlimited Sahara. If this is the case, you may not be able to buy the Jeep, but you could lease it instead.

Generally speaking, leasing is best for people with stable economic situations who know exactly what kind of driving habits they will have in the coming years. If you think your economic situation or your driving habits might be different in the future, have your sales rep review some other ownership options with you.

FINANCING USED VEHICLES VS. NEW VEHICLES

Banks have very different rules and rates for financing older cars than they do for new cars. This is because a vehicle is a depreciating asset, meaning the older it is and the more miles it has on it, the less it is worth. We will talk more about that a little later.

Because of depreciation, a used car is not as valuable as a new car to a bank or other lenders. Lenders are reluctant to allow anyone to finance a used vehicle for a long period of time because it will not retain its value as well as a new vehicle will.

A used vehicle is considered a higher risk for the borrower as well. Older cars are more likely to have unexpected, expensive repairs. Because the surprise costs may make it hard for a borrower to make the payment, there is a higher chance they will default on the loan. This is another reason banks and lenders do not finance older vehicles for a long period of time.

Banks and other lending institutions do not want to put their money into high-risk loans. Because of this, used vehicle loans tend to be for shorter terms and at higher interest rates. Newer pre-owned vehicles are typically worth more and so they have a lower risk of depreciation. They are less likely to require costly repairs or maintenance not covered by a warranty and therefore are a safer investment for the bank and a more attractive option for borrowers.

Another thing for you to consider when purchasing a vehicle is that 90% of people have to finance their vehicles; that's just a fact of most people's economic situations. Knowing how financing rates work can help you to make an informed decision. Just like a lender would not want to back a much older vehicle, you need to understand not just the cost of a used vehicle, but the maintenance and upkeep costs that can come with it. It is a common misconception that a used vehicle will have lower payments and costs associated with it. That is not always true.

WIGGLE ROOM: HOW MUCH OF A DISCOUNT CAN YOU GET?

Our experience has shown us that the average car buyer believes the markup—the profits and a salesperson's commissions on vehicles—is huge and that there are literally thousands and thousands of dollars of wiggle room in a car deal, but rarely is that true.

When it comes to mark up and wiggle room on price, it really depends on the manufacturer, what kind of vehicle it is, and whether the vehicle is new or used. It can also depend on what kind of incentives or rebates the manufacturers offer to the dealership or how expensive the car is to begin with.

Here is a general rule of thumb: the more expensive the vehicle, the more wiggle room there is. For example, a Ford Focus car has little mark up and so there isn't really any room for a discount. In contrast, there is much more mark up on a higher trim level F150 truck and therefore more chance of getting a discount.

However, that is not a hard and fast rule. Maybe you're looking at a more expensive Maserati SUV and the vehicle has been on the dealership lot for a while. The dealership has probably started discounting it so they can sell it and make room for new inventory. In this case, there probably will not be any chance of further discount even if it is a much more expensive vehicle.

Another important and unpredictable factor is what is happening in the vehicle marketplace at the time you are buying. We have seen huge fluctuations. Sometimes there is plenty of inventory with great dealer incentives and huge year-end discounts when you pretty much buy a vehicle at cost. At other times, inventory is low, and discounts are near nonexistent. At the time of writing this book, used vehicle prices are higher than we have ever seen and in fact, a truck that is a year or two old with low mileage sells for just as much as if it were new!

So, there are many variables that affect your ability to ask for a discount on the price. Now, we are not saying that you can't ever get one, but vehicle pricing is not black and white, and there are many things that account for how much room there is for negotiation.

But a dealership is a business, and they want to sell you a car. To get that sale, they may entice you with offers that seem really great, but sometimes they are not. The best deal does not always mean the cheapest deal or the lowest payment or the shortest term.

Getting the best deal is more than just getting a discount off the MSRP. We'll show you how.

TIMING CAN BE EVERYTHING

When you buy your vehicle can make a huge difference in how much you pay for it. Generally, there are three things that motivate car dealerships to give you a better deal in order to sell you a car: aged inventory, end of month, and end of year.

"Aged inventory" refers to vehicles—pre-owned vehicles, in particular—that have been on the lot a long time. Generally, a dealership puts specials on used vehicles that have been on their lot for a while. Sometimes you can get an idea of how long a vehicle has been in a dealership's inventory by paying attention to their website. There is often a filter menu at the top of the webpage that will allow you to search by age—not just by the age of the vehicle, but also by how long it's been on the lot. Additionally, if you have the time, you can watch a specific vehicle on the dealership website and track how long it's been there. Or just ask your sales professional. If you've done everything right up to this point, you are working with an honest and trustworthy sales professional who will tell you the truth. A good sales professional knows which vehicles are marked down the most.

All dealerships have monthly sales quotas that they have to hit. If the end of the month is approaching and they need to sell more vehicles to hit that quota, they will generally give a better discount in order to get the sale. This is not something they advertise or let people know about. If they really need a lot of sales, they may say something on their social media platforms about month-end specials or some other type of flash sale, but mostly they have their salespeople call their clients who are in the process of buying a vehicle to offer a better deal on the vehicle or more money for their trade-in to entice them to buy. A dealership will never tell you where they are in terms of hitting their quotas, but you can ask your sales pro for a discount, and he or she will go to the sales manager with the offer.

"Year-end" refers to the time when dealerships clear out last year's models. They are motivated to get last year's models off their lot to create room for the next year's models. The discounts can depend on the next year's model and how many changes that are made to the vehicle, but generally, models from the previous year fall under the aged inventory category, and dealers are incentivized to clear them out. These deals can result in better rates on financing, other special offers, or discounts off the prices. Whichever it turns out to be, you can usually get a much better deal on last year's model.

Dealerships also have to pay interest to the manufacturer or the bank to have new vehicles on their lot. In dealership lingo, this is called the "floorplan," and it's negotiated between the dealership and the manufacturer when they first build the dealership and then they usually re-negotiate annually or bi-annually.

Typically, a dealership gets 0% for the first 90 days that a vehicle is on their lot. However, after those 90 days, they start paying interest to have the vehicle on their lot. Therefore, dealerships are motivated to sell new vehicles as quickly as possible and want to get them off the lot in that first 90 days.

HOW TO GET THE MOST FOR YOUR TRADE

Imagine this: you are out and you see two people that look very similar, except one looks spectacular and the other not so much. In fact, the other looks a bit rough. You talk to them a bit and find out they are identical twins. What? But your first perception of one is so much better than the other. The difference? Well one probably took better care of themselves and their presentation.

Identical twins and yet . . .

This is what it is like looking at trade-ins. We see cars that come in looking immaculate. The exterior has been washed and the inside is clean. There are no wrappers, no pieces of papers, no crumbs; it's a nice-looking vehicle.

Then we get one in that looks like a family of raccoons was living in it and they took it for a joy ride through a swamp.

These two vehicles might have a very similar value. They could be the same make and be in the same mechanical condition with a comparable amount of mileage, but the one that has been poorly kept will not get as much trade-in value for two reasons. One, the dealership will have to spend a lot of money on a detail and getting the car in a condition to sell. Second, they are going to assume the worst about the rest of the vehicle and figure that if it was not even kept halfway clean that proper mechanical maintenance was neglected as well. So, they will hold back some trade money thinking it will most likely need other repairs.

So, when it comes time to trade in, make sure your vehicle is clean. If you can afford to spend a few dollars and get it detailed and properly cleaned, do it. This is especially great if the paint is not scratched as a professional wax job can make it look amazing. But, if you don't have that in your budget, give the vehicle a good clean yourself. If you're not sure how to detail your car, look on YouTube for tips on how to detail your car.

If your vehicle does need any mechanical repair or servicing, including tires or body work, don't bother to fix it before you trade in. Before a dealer takes your vehicle in on trade, they will take it for a drive and see how it feels, sounds, and drives; the results of this test drive will be a factor in how they establish the car's value, but it is doubtful that you will get enough extra money for your trade to make it worth doing the repairs beforehand.

The key to getting good value for the trade is the presentation of your trade-in vehicle. That little effort and money that you put into getting your trade looking good is the simplest and most effective way to get the best value for your trade-in.

WHAT IS MY TRADE-IN VEHICLE REALLY WORTH?

I f there is one area that seems to cause a lot of confusion for the car buyer, it is the actual value of their trade-in. Many times, we have presented clients with a dollar value and heard them say things like, "Well this dealership is offering me three thousand dollars more for my trade" or "I see the same vehicle for sale at this price" or "I looked at Kelley Blue Book and it says it is worth this much."

There are a lot of factors that determine what your trade-in is worth and also why you can be presented with conflicting offers from different places for the value of your car.

While Kelley Blue Book, the Canadian Black Book, and other guides and websites may offer a ballpark value for your car, they are not definitive and often not accurate. They give a general idea of what your vehicle could be worth. There are many other contributing factors including overall condition, how well the vehicle was cared for, the paint, the tires, the accident history, the brakes, the general supply and demand in your geographical area, and the rarity of your specific vehicle. These guides and websites cannot account for all these things.

In fact, many dealerships do not use these guides at all. They use real-time market assessment software that allows them to look at things like the number and sale price of similar cars in your area, market trends, and other factors that change on a daily, weekly, or monthly basis. A guide that estimates the price of something that experiences fluctuations in value almost daily can only tell you so much.

If you wanted to know what your vehicle is worth, a dealer can provide you with the actual cash value, or ACV, of your vehicle, which would be at the lower end of its market value. Despite the variety of trade-in values you can get at different dealerships, if you were to say to a specific dealership that you just wanted to sell your vehicle to them, they would give you the ACV and every dealership would give you a very similar value.

When a dealership simply buys your vehicle from you, there is more risk involved for them than when they take it in as a trade-in. While they are good at assessing vehicles and their values, it is not until your car goes through the shop inspection that they will know if there are any major issues they have to fix before they can sell it. This, plus other reconditioning costs, can make it hard for them to make a profit on just buying your vehicle from you and then reselling it. This is also why they will offer you the lower end of the market value of your vehicle.

But when you trade in, they have much more to gain through selling you a vehicle and so they will sweeten the deal by offering you more for your trade. Your vehicle is not worth more, but they give you that perception by taking some money out of the front end, the price of the vehicle they are selling you, and putting that towards your trade-in value. They also can do this because they can make money off of the back end of the sale with profit from financing and additional sales in the business office.

How much they can do that depends on many things like how much they need the deal to hit their quotas, how badly do they need used inventory, and how much wiggle room there is for them in the price of the vehicle you are buying. That's why you can see such a big difference from different dealerships in what you are offered for your vehicle when you trade it in.

This is called "over-allowing" for the trade and all dealerships do it. Some more than others. They will still sell you the vehicle at the original price you have agreed upon, but they will take a little less profit from the vehicle they are selling you. You actually do get a bit of a deal as they are reducing the MSRP of the vehicle you are buying and then putting that money towards your trade-in value.

This also begs the question, is it better to sell your car privately or trade it in? Of course, there is no definitive answer, and it depends on many factors like the type of car, how much you need to sell it for, and so on. One thing to consider is most people will need to finance a vehicle and so they generally make these purchases at a dealership where they can do that.

Additionally, selling your vehicle privately can be quite a hassle. Often, we have clients come back and trade in after a few months of trying to sell their cars privately. We often hear, "Man, I got tired of people saying they'd come by and then not showing up" or "People were lowballing me on price so bad" or "The buyer was making ridiculous requests like asking me to paint it first" or "I can't believe how many scammers are out there."

Another big benefit to trading in your vehicle at a dealership instead of selling it privately is the tax savings. You may have the sales professional tell you that they are giving you $10,000 for your trade-in, but if the tax rate is 7% on a new car where you live, they will say it is like getting $10,700 for your car.

This is true because when you trade in your vehicle, they subtract the value of your trade from the selling price of the vehicle you are purchasing, and you only pay taxes on the difference. So, if the vehicle you are buying is $40,000 and your trade-in is worth $10,000 then you only pay taxes on $30,000. So, you do save $700 dollars by not having to pay the additional tax. The more your trade-in is worth, the more tax you save on the vehicle you are purchasing. This could be a huge benefit to you, especially if you live in a province or state with a high tax rate.

For the majority of circumstances, it is more convenient to trade in your vehicle instead of selling it privately. If you have the time and do not need to buy a new vehicle right away, there is no harm in trying to see if you can sell it yourself for more than a dealership has offered you. Just keep in mind that the offer you were made for your trade-in may not last very long due to changing dealer programs, rebates, and market conditions.

VEHICLE DEPRECIATION

In general, a vehicle is a depreciating asset, meaning that the older it is and the more miles it has on it, the less valuable it is; however, not all vehicles depreciate the same way. The rate of depreciation can vary depending on several factors including the make and model of the vehicle, the condition it is in, and the current market conditions.

As a rule, luxury vehicles and high-end sports cars tend to depreciate faster than more affordable vehicles, as they are often more expensive to buy and to maintain. Vehicles that are known for their reliability and low maintenance costs typically depreciate more slowly, making them a more cost-effective option in the long run.

But just because a vehicle is more affordable does not mean that it will depreciate at a slower rate. There are several factors that play a part in this and the best way to look out for it is to do a bit of research into the vehicle before buying it.

This is especially important in terms of your vehicle purchasing habits. Are you more likely to keep the car for a long time and drive it until it can't be driven anymore? Or will you want to trade it in in a few years?

If you are looking to trade in after a few years and the vehicle depreciates quickly, it is easy to owe more than the vehicle is worth and be "upside down," as we call it in the auto industry. This means that when you trade in you will owe more money than the trade value of the vehicle. To avoid this, you need to make a larger down payment on your new vehicle or, much worse, roll the amount of money owing into your new vehicle purchase. This is something you want to avoid doing as it makes it very difficult to end up in a positive equity situation where your car is worth more than you owe. This is because you are not just paying for a new car, but the last one as well by adding what you owe on it onto the new car payments.

NO MONEY DOWN

No money down! Woooooo! Right? Well, maybe.

Many banks and car dealerships offer loans requiring no money down. While this might sound like a great idea, it can really hurt you financially down the road. This is because when you put no money down, you are not only financing the vehicle, you are financing the taxes on the vehicle as well.

Have you ever heard of someone who purchased a vehicle and wanted to trade it in after a few years only to find out that what they owe is more than what the car is worth? We've all heard that story, and some of us have experienced it firsthand. Typically, these stories involve people who did not put any money down when they financed their vehicle.

When you put no money down, it means most of your initial finance payments go towards tax and not the vehicle itself. As we said before, a vehicle is a depreciating asset, and the value of the vehicle depreciates the most in the first few years. If not much money is going towards the vehicle cost during that time, the value quickly becomes upside down and the person owes more on the vehicle than it is worth.

When you buy a vehicle, you have to pay tax on it just like everything else in life and because you are making a major purchase, it is a lot of tax. In the US it fluctuates between 0 and 8.3% and in Canada it varies from 5 to 20%.

For our example, let's use a tax rate of 7%. Imagine that you finance a vehicle for $35,000 with no money down. With a 7% tax rate, you actually pay $37,450 with the taxes included. In this scenario, it would be advisable to put at least $2,450 cash down to cover your taxes, so you aren't rolling them into your financing. This way you will be paying off the $35,000 vehicle price, the principal, from the start and not $37,450 including the tax. In a no money down situation, it is unlikely that you will get a 0% interest rate, so not only are you financing the taxes, but you are paying interest on them as well.

You should not finance the taxes, ever! Putting money down lowers your total cost of borrowing so that you are making payments on the vehicle itself. This will increase the likelihood that you will be in an equitable position later, meaning your vehicle is worth more than you owe on it. Otherwise, you really risk being in a negative situation, where the money you owe on your vehicle is more than its current market value.

With the popularity of loans requiring no money down, it's not surprising that so many people end up in a negative equity situation during their financing term. Now, we also understand that there are a lot of people who may not be able to afford to put any money down at the time of purchase, but there is some good news about that. Car loans are open-ended loans, meaning that there is no penalty for paying them off early. So, even if you can't put money down at the time of purchase, you can get yourself ahead by putting more money toward the payment later. We have seen this many times where people use their tax returns, money owed to them, inheritance, or whatever extra money comes in later to help offset the fact that they did not put money down at the beginning. The real problem is that many people do not understand the potential consequences of putting no money down and never do anything to offset the risks.

ZERO-PERCENT FINANCING

It's big! It's enticing! It's zero-percent financing! But is it a good deal?

Have you noticed that when manufacturers offer 0% interest, they never offer big discounts as well? This is because lending institutions never loan money for free. It costs money to borrow money, so how can dealerships offer 0% financing?

When a car manufacturer offers 0% financing, they pay money to the banks and lenders to lower the rate all the way down to 0%. This means that the dealership is offering to subsidize or "subvent" a portion of the financing costs for a car loan, and this cuts into their profits. Because of this cost, they don't combine big discounts and 0% at the same time. It's always one or the other.

Ford is a great example of this. We have seen Ford offer their customers "employee-pricing" discounts in the summer and big "year-end" discounts in late fall through early winter. Then they go heavy on advertising 0% interest financing in the spring and early fall months. They never do big discounts with 0% financing at the same time.

So, which is best for you? 0% financing or a big discount? Well, it depends on how long you plan to keep your vehicle while financing it.

So how long do you want to finance for? Two years? Five years? Eight years?

If you answered anywhere between two and three years, then you should not take 0% financing. You should wait until the manufacturer offers a bigger discount. The reason is that if you trade in every few years like some people do, you will be further ahead on your trade-in value on a vehicle that you paid less for at the start. So rather than 0% financing, go for a year-end deal or other big discount when the price is reduced.

If you are going to finance for five or more years and can get 0% financing, take advantage of that. Though usually we see that 0% is only offered up to about a four-year financing term. As far as something like an eight-year term, it is highly unlikely you will get 0% financing, and we really do not recommend financing a vehicle for that long. With such a lengthy term for payments, it is easy to be upside down if you need to trade in or sell the vehicle before the end of the finance term. Also, your warranties most likely will have expired before your payments are done; manufacturer warranties can differ quite a bit in time and millage and it is not good to still be making payments and have no warranty left. Then you risk a costly repair cost on top of your financing payment and this may cause you to miss a car payment and hurt your credit.

If you want to trade in your vehicle after a few years, it is easier to have more equity at trade-in time if you got a big discount at the beginning. Equity means the current trade-in value is more than you owe on the vehicle.

We talked about negative equity, or being upside down on your trade in value, and there is more chance of this happening when you purchase at a higher price and at 0% financing and want to trade in after a few years. If you put no money down, then your situation could be even worse.

But if you get a good price on the vehicle at sale time, put some money down, and don't finance for a long term, even if you pay a higher interest rate, you will be in a much better place than you would be in a 0% financing situation.

IT'S OK TO SHOP FOR VEHICLES, BUT NOT FOR FINANCING

Here is an important note: when you are in the process of looking for a sales professional and a vehicle, some dealerships will offer to run a credit check to see if you qualify for the vehicle that you are interested in. Please don't do any credit applications until you have chosen your sales professional and the vehicle you want.

Sometimes clients are not sure about their credit or do not understand how applying for credit works. Often a salesperson will say, "Let's run your credit and see what you qualify for." Now this is not really a bad thing, but when that person goes to a few different dealerships and does this over and over, it looks like they are shopping for credit and not a vehicle. This raises a red flag with banks and lenders and may decrease your ability to qualify for a loan.

So please, wait until you have at least found your sales professional before running any credit checks. We have run credit checks for people who were not sure how good their credit might be, or even if they would qualify, to prevent them from getting all excited about a great new ride and then finding out later that they could not get financing for it. This is the only time we say it's OK to fill out a credit application before picking a vehicle.

PART FOUR

Your Credit and the Business Office

When you have selected the vehicle you want to buy the sales manager, or the sales pro in a hybrid position, will present you with rate and term options—the amount of money you will pay monthly or bi-weekly for so many years. The rates and terms will vary depending on several things, like how long you take to pay for your vehicle, if you make payments monthly or bi-weekly, and interest rates.

Once you have agreed to a rate and term, you will then go into the business office where the business manager will run your credit. If you are buying a used vehicle they will shop for the best interest rates and loan terms with lenders for you. With new vehicles the rates are set by the manufacturer. Sometimes the business manager will come up with different terms and rates if it turns out the borrower's credit is not as good as they thought it was.

Aside from setting up financing through lenders for you, a finance manager will try to sell you "back-end" products. These are things like maintenance and protection packages as well as extended warranties. Just like many things, they may or may not be a fit for your vehicle-buying habits. So, we are going to talk about them a bit, and you can decide if they are appropriate for you.

We'll also talk a bit about the basics of credit, so that you have an understanding of terms and things the business manager will tell you. But, most of all, we want to help you make a decision that will protect your future credit and finances.

Something important we'd like to touch on is a common thing we see some buyers do. That is paying attention to only the payment and not considering the term or interest rates. We get that most people are budget conscious and so often they only focus on the payment. But, a low payment over a long period can mean a lot of interest and that can be a lot of money. Also with bi-weekly payments, there are 26 payments a year vs. 12 with monthly so while the payments are a lower amount, there are more of them.

A simple way to get a perspective on this is to calculate the total you will make in payments by simply multiplying the payment amount with how many payments you will make over the term, and then subtract the cost of the vehicle, taxes and fees. For example if the payments are 700 dollars a month for four years, 700 x 12 x 4 = $33,600. If the vehicle is $30,500 with taxes and fees then you know you are paying $3,100 in interest.

I did this with a client once and she found that by tightening her budget a bit and paying 150 dollars more a month, she saved close to two thousand dollars in interest. It's little things like this, plus making the best purchase decision based on your vehicle buying habits where you can save thousands and thousands of dollars.

CREDIT PROGRESSION

C redit progression may be one of the most important factors in helping you qualify for a vehicle-financing loan. Credit progression refers to the amount of credit that you have had over a certain period of time.

As an example, most people start off with a cell phone plan and a credit card. Your cell phone plan may only be a couple hundred dollars and your credit card may have a limit of only $1,000. So, in building your "credit progression," you have proven that you can handle approximately $1,200 in available credit or potential bills each month.

The problem comes when you then try to finance a $50,000 vehicle. You haven't proven that you can handle a loan that size yet and unless you have an incredible debt-servicing ratio, meaning you make a lot of money and have not had lots of credit in the past, you will get denied. A perfect example is my young coworker who bought a very expensive truck once he started to make good money. Otherwise, why would a bank lend you $50,000 when you've only ever handled $1,200 or less in credit?

Simply put, as a starting point, don't try to borrow more money than you make in income each year. Whatever credit has been lent to you, don't max it out. Try to keep it around 30%. Then build gradually. Start with a cell phone plan and a credit card with a low limit. Then ask for an increase in your limit on that credit card or get a second credit card. Then buy a $20,000–$30,000 vehicle and make all of your payments on time. Then, later, trade that car in and buy a $30,000–$40,000 vehicle and make all of your payments on time. Then, later, trade that car in and buy a car worth $50,000 or more and make all of your payments on time. This is called credit progression.

This way you will also not overextend yourself on your car payments and start hating the car you should love.

CREDIT UTILIZATION

Credit utilization is a measure of how much of your available credit you are currently using. It is calculated by dividing the total amount of credit you are using by the total amount of credit available to you. For example, if you have a credit card with a $10,000 limit and you have a balance of $2,500, your credit utilization would be 25%.

Credit utilization is important because it is one of the factors that credit scoring models take into account when determining your credit score. Generally, the lower your credit utilization, the better it is for your credit score and overall ability to get approved for a loan. A low credit utilization indicates that you are using a small portion of your available credit, which suggests that you are managing your credit responsibly. On the other hand, a high credit utilization means that you are using a large portion of your available credit, which can be a red flag for lenders and can negatively impact your credit score.

A common suggestion is to keep your credit utilization below 30%. This means if you have a credit card with a $10,000 limit, you should try to keep your balance below $3,000.

Our best advice is don't max out your credit cards and personal lines of credit. Just because a bank or credit card company is willing to give you credit does not mean you should use all of it. Just use some of it. Try to keep it at 30%.

You might wonder, "What if you keep it at 0%?" In other words, what if you have available credit, but you never use it? That's not good either. When you are considering borrowing money to buy a vehicle, the banks will want to see your track record with using credit in a healthy manner. Never using your available credit means the banks have no evidence that you can handle credit in a responsible manner. You need to use your available credit in order to build "good credit."

DEBT SERVICE RATIO

Something important to understand when financing a vehicle is the debt service ratio, or DSR.

The DSR is a financial measure that compares the borrower's monthly income to their monthly debt payments. It is typically expressed as a percentage and is used by lenders to determine a borrower's ability to repay their loans.

A low DSR indicates that a borrower has a high level of income relative to their debt obligations and is therefore less likely to default on the loan. A high DSR, on the other hand, indicates that a borrower has a low level of income relative to their debt obligations and is therefore more likely to default on the loan. Lenders typically require a certain DSR for car loans, and borrowers with a DSR above the required threshold may be denied the loan or offered a higher interest rate.

Something that we often see is someone wanting to finance a car with a purchase price or payment obligations above what they should be committing to.

And we can understand how it might happen. When you first find your car, you fall in love with the features and style of it. Then there is an initial honeymoon period. It's like the beginning of a romance! You love it, take pictures with it, drive it places, and go exploring. When you get the right vehicle and the right payments, that feeling will last. But, if you overcommit on your payments and end up with a bad DSR, the romance will fade, and resentment will grow. It's like the example in the beginning of this book with my young coworker who overextended himself and ended up feeling owned by his truck. While a good sales professional may caution you, the truth is it is your decision. Be responsible.

There are two things we do not want to happen to you: the first is that you make a purchase that hurts your credit long term; the second is that you end up resenting your car. We want you to be happy with your purchase for years to come.

MAINTENANCE PLANS

Maintenance plans are typically sold by the business manager or the finance manager when you are purchasing a new vehicle. They are sometimes offered on newer pre-owned vehicles, but it's most common for maintenance plans to be offered on new vehicle purchases.

A maintenance plan allows you to pre-purchase your vehicle's maintenance. Typically, four-year, five-year, and six-year options are available. By purchasing a maintenance plan, you are typically saving yourself a bit of time and money by buying all or most of your maintenance upfront.

Say you opt for a five-year maintenance plan. You save money because it allows you to pay off the cost of the maintenance plan across a five-year period instead of having maintenance bills. Typically, it ends up being less expensive than if you were to add up all of your maintenance costs at the end of a five-year period. Additionally, a good maintenance plan will offer the use of loaner vehicles or pick-up and drop-off services when you need work done on your car.

Maintenance plans are definitely worth considering. However, they are most valuable for people who typically keep their new vehicles for at least four to six years. The cost of maintenance in your first two years of ownership should be minimal: a few oil changes, fluid top ups, and tire rotations. It's not until years three through six that maintenance starts to become more expensive as you are going to have to consider things like brake jobs, flushes, and suspension work. So, if you plan to trade in after only two to three years, a maintenance plan is not really going to be worth it to you.

Another side benefit to pre-paid maintenance plans is that you can almost always add them to your financing or leasing plan. Imagine that you buy a new car and finance it for five years. New vehicles typically have lower interest rates than pre-owned vehicles do. So, you could add a maintenance plan to the total cost of your financing and pay it off over five years. During that five-year time period that you are paying off your vehicle, all of the maintenance is covered, and you'll also have a manufacturer warranty during most or maybe even the entire time. That's an easy ownership experience that comes with a lot of peace of mind.

WARRANTIES AND PROTECTION PACKAGES: ARE THEY WORTH IT OR NOT?

Warranties and protection packages are generally sold by the business office. They are typically pitched during the loan approval process or when you are finalizing the details with the business manager.

Warranties and protection packages are worth your consideration; however, they are not all the same and whether they're appropriate really depends on how you plan to use your new vehicle. Generally speaking, we compare purchasing warranties and protection packages to buying car insurance. It depends on a variety of factors including how long you plan to keep your car, how much driving you'll be doing, what type of driving you'll be doing, and how much of a deductible you want.

Extended warranties and protection packages can be purchased on most new and pre-owned vehicles. Although the options and coverages may vary slightly depending on the age of the vehicle.

Extended warranties are exactly what they sound like. They are an extension of the vehicle manufacturer's warranty. Are they worth it? It depends. They are definitely worth your consideration, but what if you typically trade your vehicle in every four to five years? Well, then the manufacturer's warranty should suffice, and an extended warranty will likely not be worth the extra money.

If you are financing for a long period of time, like five to eight years, then extended warranties are something to consider. We talked a bit about how your powertrain and comprehensive warranties can expire long before you pay off your vehicle and if something goes wrong you could be paying an expensive repair bill on top of your payment. So if you are financing and your comprehensive and powertrain warranties expire long before your payments end, they can be a good investment.

Protection packages are also exactly what they sound like. They can be comprised of different products from a variety of after-market companies. They can include, but are not limited to, interior leather or fabric protection, paint protection films, paint protection coatings, rust protection, undercoat, and windshield warranties. The reason they are often called protection packages is because the business manager will typically bundle a few items together that are complementary to each other. You may get a better deal by purchasing a few products at once.

Are protection packages worth it? Again, it depends on how long you plan to keep your vehicle and how you plan to use it. It also depends on the climate where you live and what environmental factors may degrade your vehicle over time. If you live in Canada, like us, most of these protection products are a very worthwhile consideration.

Children and pets are also something to take into consideration when looking at protection packages. When I had clients who had pets and young children I recommended getting the rears seat protected. Both children and pets are adorable, but messy. Buying protection packages can save your interior or exterior from excessive wear and increase the trade value.

INSURANCE

This is the final stage prior to taking ownership of your car; your sales pro will have you sit down with an auto insurance rep to set up insurance for your vehicle. In some dealerships, the finance manager may also set up insurance, but the majority of dealerships work with outside auto insurance agencies that send reps to the dealership when needed.

Car insurance is a complex topic that could be a book in itself. There are so many different options and rules that vary from state to state and province to province, we couldn't hope to cover it all here. Suffice to say, a good insurance agent, just like a good sales pro, should go through your wants and needs and help you make a selection that fits your lifestyle.

PART FIVE

Taking Ownership and After the Purchase

Congrats! You are about to drive away in your new vehicle. Before you take ownership of your vehicle, the sales pro will have it all cleaned up for you and ready to take home.

This is your last chance to do a proper walk around your vehicle and make sure everything is OK. If it is a new car, look for things like scratches in the paint and any dings or dents. If it is used, it may already come with a few, but you need to check over your new purchase carefully at this time. If you see something later, it might be difficult to prove to the dealership that it did not happen after you drove the car off the lot.

This is also when the sales pro will go through all the features and functions of your new car with you. In the car sales industry, they often call this "taking delivery." This should include pairing your phone and setting up any brand services like Chevrolet has with Onstar or Ford has with Fordpass.

There is a ton of technology in new vehicles and, depending on the trim level, the features might involve anything from basic safety and comfort technology to more complex options like adaptive cruise control and massage seats. Remember, at this point, you will have bought your vehicle, negotiated terms with the sales manager, spent time in the business office, and also organized your insurance. So, it can be hard to take it all the features of your new vehicle after all that.

A good sales pro knows this, and they should offer to set up a second appointment about a week or two after you have had the vehicle.

This gives you time to try out all the features of your vehicle and then come back to your sales pro with any questions that you might have. It is also nice because, since you will be fresher, you will be able to take in all the information about your new vehicle's features better. There are some pretty cool features in new vehicles and there are many custom settings and preferences your sales pro can explain to you and help you program.

CONCLUSION

Congratulations!

You are now armed with the knowledge we have gained over decades of experience in the car industry, and you are well-equipped to make a solid purchasing decision when buying your next car from a dealership.

This is important to us as we want your next car-purchasing experience to be the best it can be.

Not only that, but we want to make sure you are truly getting the best deal and setting up your credit and finances for long-term success.

Now that we have helped you, help us back. Make sure to leave a review for us wherever you purchased this book so that we can carry on helping others.

Sincerely,
Phil Mendzat and Ryan Leverette

If there is something you need more help with or would like more information about, we'd love to hear from you.

Insidercarguide@gmail.com